The Darkness Descended

Danielle Chartier

BookLeaf Publishing

Presentation by *BookLeaf Publishing*

Web: www.bookleafpub.com

E-mail: info@bookleafpub.com

ISBN: 9789357211420

First edition 2022

DEDICATION

I dedicate this collection of poems to the beautiful souls of all those unjustly crucified.

ACKNOWLEDGEMENT

I would like to acknowledge every person, known and unknown to me, involved in assisting on this healing journey. My sincerest thanks for your kindness.

PREFACE

6 years ago, one moment, changed everything. The poems in this book are parts of my journey of healing.

A Wish on Your Birthday

Focus: The Fool (Card 0/22)
Themes: Innocence, Risk, Beginnings

If I only knew
that was my last moment with you
I would have snuggled you a little longer
Held you tighter
My arms around you a bit stronger
I'm not sure how we lost you Or why
I often sit and think about before
and sometimes I cry
because the brother I knew is dead
The sweet, smiley little guy
with the curly brown head
Life is so different now
Those years a distant memory...
Lost
I was not prepared for the enormous cost
Of growing older
If I had a chance to step back
One chance...
Redo...
any moment of that life...
I would choose the last night at home
Those last few hours, cozied-up
Watching a movie with you

"Just Hang-in There"

Focus: The Fool (Card 0/22)
Themes: Innocence, Risk, Beginnings

"Never Lose Your Childish Innocence"
Words permanent upon my skin
Savagely ripped from my flesh!
Words of Hope, now possessed
The phrase, a whip in the hand of my faceless captor
Relentless taunting
Every lash a new brand berndt into my raw, bloody back
Crack! Crack! Crack!
Punishment
No Crime
Madness all around me
I see no escape
My knees buckle
I wail in agony!
I look to the Heavens
One cotton ball cloud smiles back at me

Manifest

Focus: The Magician (Card 1)
Themes: Action, Creativity, Success

Born with the secret
Magic once familiar
Foreign to this soul

Seeing the Invisible

Focus: The High Priestess (Card 2)
Themes: Secrets, Wisdom, The Spiritual World

I can see the veil on days when it's thin
I can hear voices softly calling my name in the wind
I smell the aroma of places I've never stepped-in or been
I can feel your pain
I can relate to your sin

I am sort of a bridge between here and there
I've lived, I've died
My experience, truly rare

I observe more than most
It's difficult to explain
Most days I feel lonely, isolated, insane

I pray for a partner who can accept fully
With no judgement
A life, happily, we can share
Because many days being me,
is extremely exhausting, hard to bear.

With you, I am home

Focus: The Empress (Card 3)
Themes: Abundance, generosity, Creativity, Wife, Female Aspect

Empress, Daleth, the door
Emperor, Hei, the window
Two aspects
Of the same soul, man and wife
Together they conceive
Their seeds create a new life

Words spoken without sound...

Focus: The Emperor (Card 4)
Themes: Control, Security, Order, Ambition, Husband, Male Aspect

Hey
I haven't seen you in so long
I've missed you every moment I've been gone
I'm not sure where to start
I know I broke your heart
With these stupid games
I have so much to tell you, so much to explain
I know my explanation doesn't compare to the pain
you have endured
You have suffered every day
I know the cost that you paid
I did try to fix you...

I really miss you, did I say that?
I think so...
There are so many things I need you to know

Like...
You did nothing wrong

You are amazing, beautiful and so incredibly strong!
Back then it was crazy
The feelings I felt for you...

Gosh...did I mention you amaze me?
Yes, I think so...
These are things I just really need you to know.

Please don't cry
I hate that I had to lie
If you'll let me
I want a chance to let you see
For yourself
Who I really am
Who I want to be

I want the honor of being your husband
I want the honor of you as my wife
I want us to start a family
Walk hand-in-hand
Together, love, let's build our life

I love you with all of my heart
I know you love me too
Please spend the rest of your life with me
Please say you will
Please say "I do"

A Vau (Kindness) from Above

Focus: The Hierophant (Card 5)
Themes: Education, Unity, Spiritual Direction

A prayer that He would send help
Healing is needed
The prayer was answered today

It just feels right...

Focus: The Hierophant (Card 5)
Themes: Education, Unity, Spiritual Direction

Your lips on my lips
Your strong hands grip my hips

Pull me close
I softly kiss and nibble
Making the most
Of my journey down your chest
Follow the trail

I kneel
My eyes intently look-up into yours
The energy from your fingertips
Anticipation pours
I feel your body tremble
As I part my lips

Pure ecstasy crosses your face
As I savor my first taste
I take my time, slowly at first
Then intensity builds as I pick-up the pace

You can't wait one more minute

Before I know it, I'm on my back
You're thrust up in it

Seconds before separate
Now rhythmically in-sync
Our breathing heavy, sweat dripping
A heavenly link
The space you entered, tightly gripping
To the source of this pleasure

Hold-on to the feeling
The endless Ohhh....
The passion has peaked
One last thrust
You explode!

The Power of Words

Focus: The Lovers (Card 6)
Themes: Love and Relationships, Maturity, Decisions

"Just be naked with me"
5 words that healed 30 years
Of insecurity, abuse and tears

The Chariot

Focus: The Chariot (Card 7)
Themes: Determination, Victory, Journey

Swing Low
So I can see you
Sweet Chariot
Come forth, please appear
The time has come
To carry on and find my way home
Please help me on my journey
Protect and keep me safe
Help me to stay strong
And to hold tight to my faith
Remind me that my steadfast
determination will see me through
To the end
To the victory
Divine love will not forsake you

Strength

Focus: Strength (Card 8)
Themes: Patience, Tension, Courage

All these years
All these tears

I wish I knew the purpose

All these tests
All the best

Of me, by now I'd think it would surface

Someday I'll know
The truth will show

The lies and deceit of the two-faced

Permission

Focus: The Hermit (Card 9)
Themes: Healing and Self-Exploration

You are deeply hurt
AND
It is okay to smile again

Fate

Focus: The Wheel of Fortune (Card 10)
Themes: Fate, Destiny, Change, Intuition

All that defined me
I lost everything
My identity

The only thing not lost
Was my faith
I had to hold tight to it
No matter the cost

What is the destiny I now own?
I feel it inside of me
Deep in my bones

I almost feel
That this tragedy was my fate
I had to experience
The discrimination and hate

To assist me in handling the load
That which lies ahead
Somewhere down the road.

It works itself out

Focus: Justice (Card 11)
Themes: Balance, Perception, Objectivity

Karma
Invisible Justice
Restores Balance
No Discrimination
All are equal
Our deeds good or bad
Adjustments are made
Puts order back in place

The Hanging Man

Focus: The Hanging Man (Card 12)
Themes: Waiting, Sacrifice, Enlightenment

How am I supposed to be free?
When I am left with a prison of questions
Shackled by the unknown

Death

Focus: Death (Card 13)
Themes: Transformation, Change

So many Endings and Beginnings
Transformations abound
It's unclear
Who lives here
Who inhabits this body now?
A familiar face
A much slower pace
Constant tense and furrowed brow

Temperance

Focus: Temperance (Card 14)
Themes: Moderation, Reconciliation, Healing, Angelic Guidance

My patience wears thin
If love is to win
Where the fuck have you been!?

With each passing day
More hope slips away
Don't know what to say...

I've not heard
Any news, not a word
My feelings are becoming blurred

That is what scares me the most
One day you'll be free
To make your way back to me
Anticipation
Excitement of again being close

I'll be filled with hate
From all the pain
All the years I had to wait

Just to see you again

We'll both die alone
Longing for the home
We found in eachother, by fate

The Devil

Focus: The Devil (Card 15)
Themes: Enslavement, Temptation

Overturning Roe Vs. Wade
Is just the beginning
Of a slippery slope
That none of us escapes unscathed

Collapse

Focus: The Tower (Card 16)
Themes: Destruction and Enlightenment

I've never fought so hard
for something I believe in
I did everything I could possibly do
to show you
I still had to let you go
Everything always goes
There is not one thing in life that I have loved
That I have gotten to keep
Why would you be any different?
I wish I had your "perspective"
All I see right now is devastation

The Star

Focus: The Star (Card 17)
Themes: Hope, Guidance, Inspiration, Creativity

Inspiration helps me through the day
Keeps my mind busy, focused on projects
Using discarded treasures, chalk-paint and
air-dry clay.

Some days I have enough energy to create a
piece of my own
Other days I'm just learning
Absorbing heaps of content from my phone

I know when it is right
My time will come
I will no longer have to fight
The outside pressure to conform

I'll be free to source, design and make
Creativity overflowing
No longer a "happy face" that is fake

Darkness Descended

Focus: The Moon
Themes: Illusion, Dreams, Crisis

Darkness descended
that morning
It was storming
I started to cry
As I kissed you goodbye
You teared-up too
I didn't know then
But I know now
It's because you knew
My life would end
Within an hour or two

9:21 on 9/21
Is when I ran out the door
Something just clicked in my brain
in the middle of the store
That decision to flee, in that moment
I chose you instead of choosing me
The life I knew was over
Who I was, was no more

To all involved in this elaborate lie

And to those who, going on 6 years, have kept it
alive
Was it worth it...are you satisfied?
Have you ever regretted your part
In breaking me and watching me die?

www.ingramcontent.com/pod-product-compliance
Lightning Source LLC
Chambersburg PA
CBHW051755130826
49812CB00033B/1163
* 9 7 8 9 3 5 7 2 1 1 4 2 0 *